Table of Con
Phonics
Level 1

M000117240

Consonant Letters

Hi! I'm Buddy - your good reading bear. Follow my directions to be a terrific reader.

Match the consonant letter on the block to one on the right side.

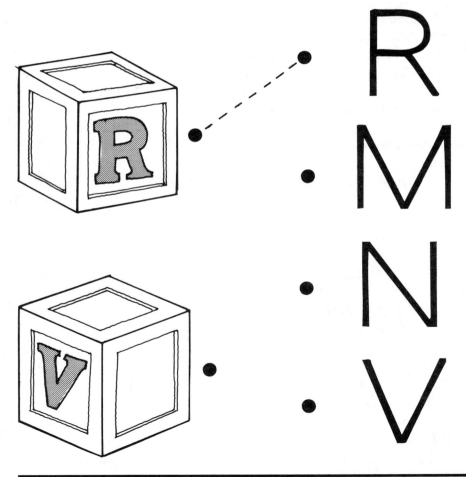

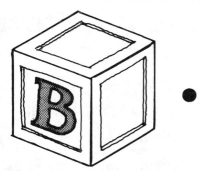 •

• S

 •

• K

• B

 •

• N

 •

Consonant Letters

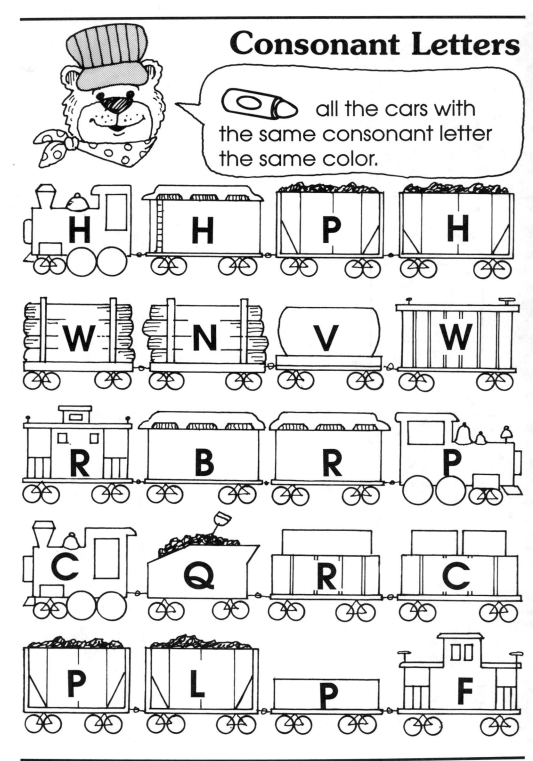

all the cars with the same consonant letter the same color.

Connect the trains with the same letter.

Consonant Letters

Make these beach balls pretty. 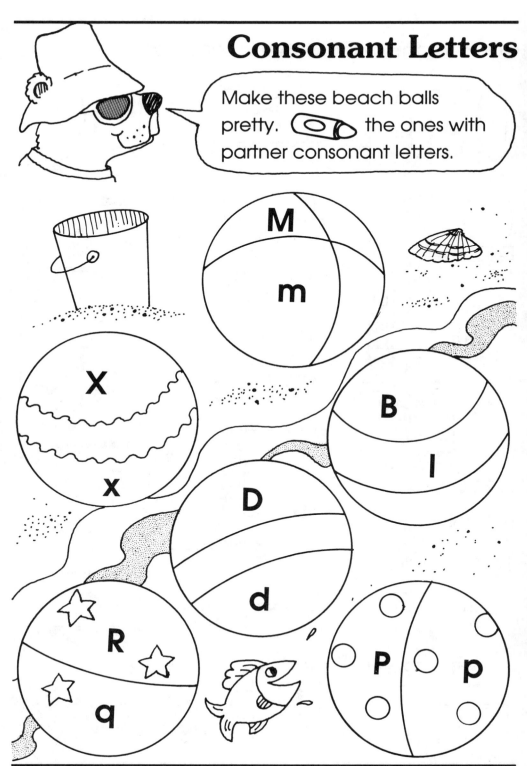 the ones with partner consonant letters.

M
m

X
x

B
l

D
d

R
q

P
p

6

Make pretty beach towels. 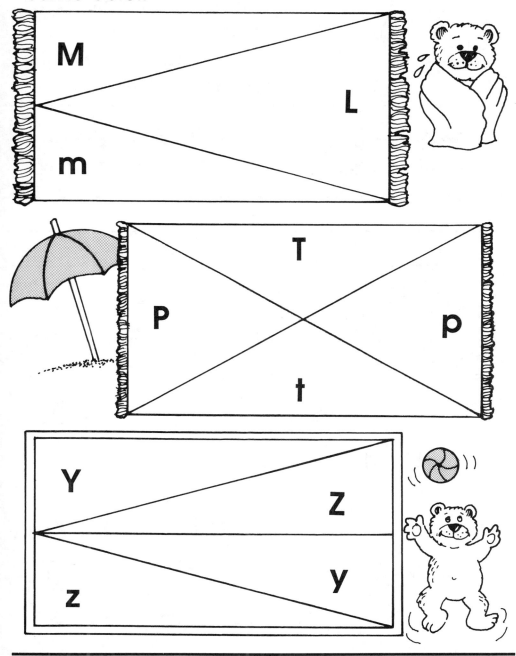 the triangles with partner consonant letters the same color.

M

m

L

T

P

p

t

Y

Z

z

y

7

Sounds B and C

Listen for the beginning consonant letter. ✏ _ the letters. 🖍 the pictures that begin with the sound like 🐝 .

B b   B b

C c   C c

the pictures that begin with the sound like 🐄.

Sound D and Review

 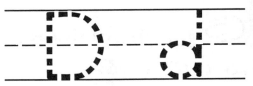

I love things that begin with **d** - like **d**oughnuts.

D d D d

 the pictures that begin with the sound

like  .

✏️ _ the large and small consonant letters each picture begins with under the picture.

B b

✏️◯ the letters that are the same.

B		d
	(D)	
D		C

c		B
	(c)	
D		C

Sounds F and G

Please meet my **f**ine **f**eathered **f**riend!

F f

Ff

the pictures that begin with the sound like .

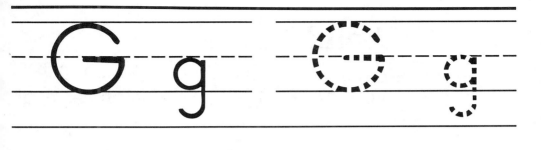

the things in the picture that begin with the sound like 👻 .

Sound H and Review

H makes me feel **h**appy!

✏️ the pictures that start with **h**!

 a line from the letters to a picture which begins with that consonant sound.

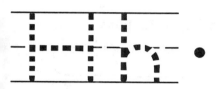 •

•

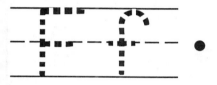 •

•

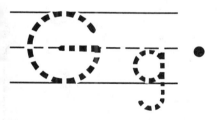 •

•

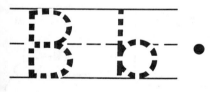 •

•

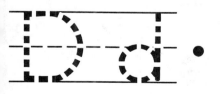 •

•

Review B, C, D, F, G, H

Match the cookies with the matching jars.

b

D

h

B

c

C

F

g

d

H

f

G

___ a line from the candles to the correct cupcakes. Match the large and small letters.

Review B, C, D, F, G, H

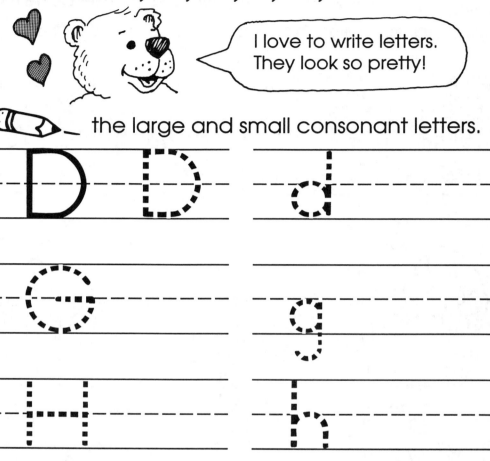

I love to write letters. They look so pretty!

_____ the large and small consonant letters.

 the pictures. 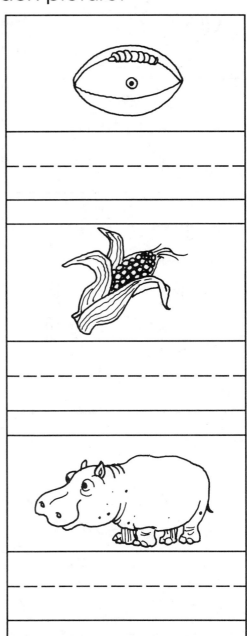 the beginning consonant letter under each picture.

Review B, C, D, F, G, H

Color the pictures. Trace the beginning consonant letter under each picture.

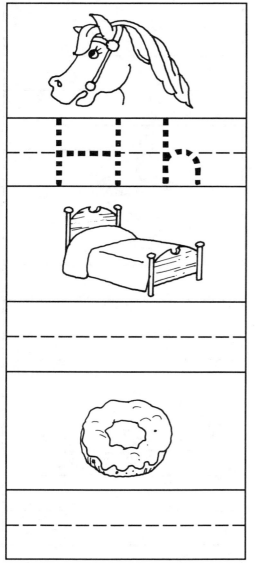

Hh

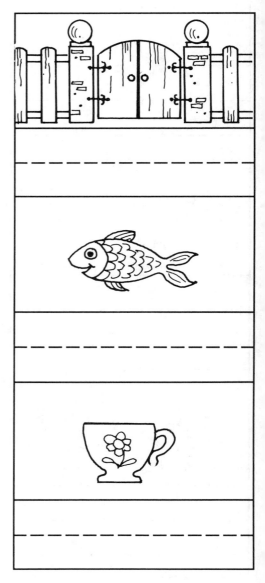

 your own pictures that begin with each letter.

f

d

g

h

c

b

Sounds J and K

I love jack-in-the-boxes!

J j   

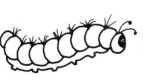 the pictures that begin with the sound like  .

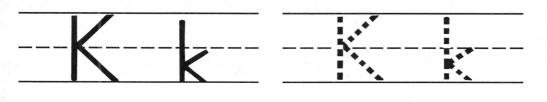

the picture that begins with the sound
like

Sound L and Review

I love lollipops!

the pictures that begin with the sound

like 🍭 .

 the consonant letters that sound like the pictures in each box. 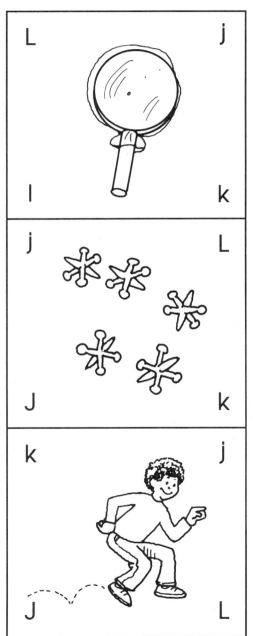 the pictures.

K		k
L		J

L		j
l		k

j		k
J		K

j		L
J		k

L		j
K		l

k		j
J		L

Sounds M and N

Meet my friend
Munchy **M**ouse.

M m   M m

the pictures that begin with the sound
like 🐭 .

N n   N n

the pictures that begin with the sound like 9 .

Sound P and Review

Peter **P**iper
ate a **p**eck of
pickled **p**eppers.

P p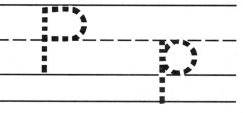

the pictures that begin with the sound
like ![pig] .

the correct consonant letter under each picture.

_ _ _ _ _ _ _ _ _ _

_ _ _ _ _ _ _ _ _ _

_ _ _ _ _ _ _ _ _ _

Review J, K, L, M, N, P

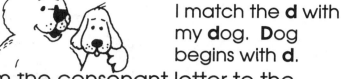

I match the **d** with my **d**og. **D**og begins with **d**.

_ from the consonant letter to the picture whose name begins with the consonant letter. the picture.

Sounds Q and R

Grandma just made this **quilt** for me!

Q q

the pictures that begin with the sound like

SSSHHH

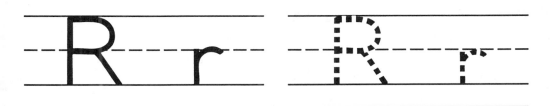

the pictures that begin with the sound like .

Sound S and Review

I just made a **super s**andwich!

S s   S s

the pictures that begin with the sound like ☀.

_ the beginning consonant letter under each picture. the pictures.

Sounds T and V

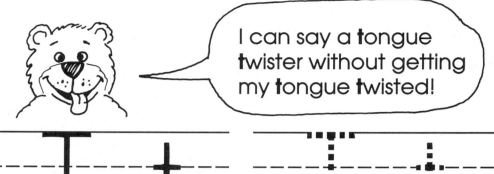

I can say a tongue twister without getting my tongue twisted!

the pictures that begin with the sound like

Tutor's Guide

This Tutor's Guide contains answer keys for Phonics Level 1. Pull it out from the book to use as a guide.

Consonant Letters

Hi! I'm Buddy - your good reading bear. Follow my directions to be a terrific reader.

Match the consonant letter on the block to one on the right side.

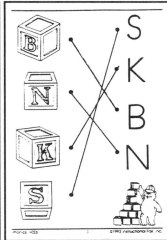

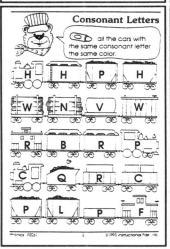

Consonant Letters

(color) all the cars with the same consonant letter the same color.

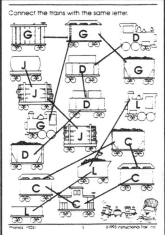

Connect the trains with the same letter.

Consonant Letters

Make these beach balls pretty. (color) the ones with partner consonant letters.

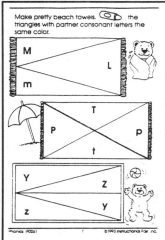

Make pretty beach towels. (color) the triangles with partner consonant letters the same color.

Sounds B and C

Listen for the beginning consonant letter. (circle) the letters. (circle) the pictures that begin with the sound like (book).

(circle) the pictures that begin with the sound like (cat).

Sound D and Review

I love things that begin with d - like doughnuts.

D d   D d
D d   D d

the pictures that begin with the sound like

the large and small consonant letters each picture begins with under the picture.

B b   D d
C c   C c
B b   D d

the letters that are the same.

| B | D | d |
| D | | C |

| C | C | B |
| D | | C |

Sounds F and G

Please meet my fine feathered friend!

F f   F f
F f   F f

the pictures that begin with the sound like

G g   G g
G g   G g

the things in the picture that begin with the sound like

Sound H and Review

H makes me feel happy!

the pictures that start with h!

H h   H h
H h
H h
H h

a line from the letters to a picture which begins with that consonant sound.

H h
F f
G g
B b
D d

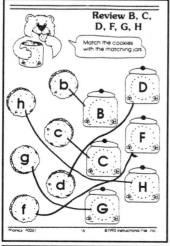

Review B, C, D, F, G, H

Match the cookies with the matching jars.

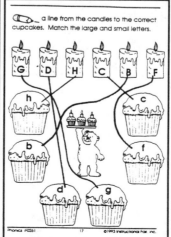

a line from the candles to the correct cupcakes. Match the large and small letters.

Review B, C, D, F, G, H

I love to write letters. They look so pretty!

the large and small consonant letters.

D D   d d
G G   g g
H H   h h
B B   b b
C C   c c

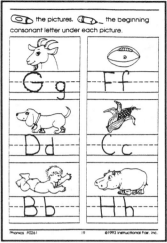

🖍 the pictures. 🖍_ the beginning consonant letter under each picture.

G g F f
D d C c
B b H h

Review B, C, D, F, G, H

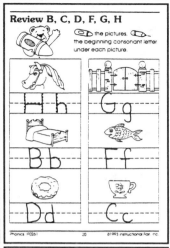

🖍 the pictures. 🖍_ the beginning consonant letter under each picture.

H h G g
B b F f
D d C c

🖍_ your own pictures.

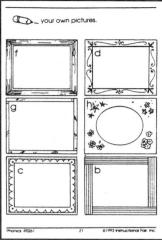

f   d
g   h
c   b

Sounds J and K

I love jack-in-the-boxes!

J j J j

🖍 the pictures that begin with the sound like 🚙

K k K k
K k K k

🖍 the picture that begins with the sound like 🔑

Sound L and Review

I love lollipops!

L l L l

🖍 the pictures that begin with the sound like 🍭

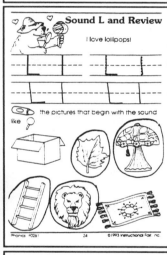

🖍 the consonant letters that sound like the pictures in each box. 🖍 the pictures.

K k
L j
L J
j k
j L
J K
J k
L j
k j
K l
J L

Sounds M and N

Meet my friend Munchy Mouse.

M m M m
M m M m

🖍 the pictures that begin with the sound like 🐑

N n N n
N n N n

🖍 the pictures that begin with the sound like 👃

Tutor's Guide IF0261   C   ©1993 Instructional Fair, Inc.

Sound P and Review

Peter Piper ate a peck of pickled peppers.

P p P p
P p P p

the pictures that begin with the sound like

the correct consonant letter under each picture.

P p   J j
M m   L l
N n   K k

Review J, K, L, M, N, P

I match the d with my dog. Dog begins with d.

from the consonant letter to the picture whose name begins with the consonant letter. the picture.

N   J
K
M
M   N

k
k
j   k
m   p

Sounds Q and R

Grandma just made this quilt for me!

Q q   Q q
Q q   Q q

the pictures that begin with the sound like

R r   R r
R r   R r

the pictures that begin with the sound like

Good work!

Sound S and Review

I just made a super sandwich!

S s   S s
S s   S s

the pictures that begin with the sound like

the beginning consonant letter under each picture. the pictures.

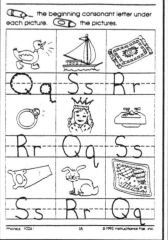

Q q   S s   R r
R r   Q q   S s
S s   R r   Q q

Sounds T and V

I can say a tongue twister without getting my tongue twisted!

T t   T t

the pictures that begin with the sound like

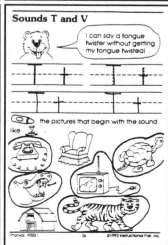

V v V v V v

___ the pictures that begin with the sound like [heart]

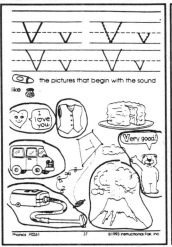

Sound W and Review

I'm looking through a wide window!

W w W w W w

___ the pictures that begin with the sound like [wagon]

___ each large and small consonant letter.
___ a line to the picture that begins with that sound.

S s
T t
V v
S s
W w
R r
W w
Q q

Sounds X and Y

Let's see. The only word I can think of that begins with x is x-ray.

X x X x X x

When you go to the dentist, you get an

x-ray

If you break your arm, the doctor takes an

x-ray

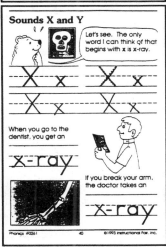

Y y Y y

___ the pictures that begin with the sound like [yo-yo]

Whew! You worked hard!

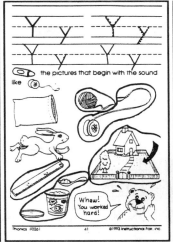

Sound Z and Review

Z is the last letter in the alphabet! Let's celebrate by going to the zoo!

Z z Z z Z z

___ the pictures that begin with the sound like [zipper]

___ the beginning consonant letter.

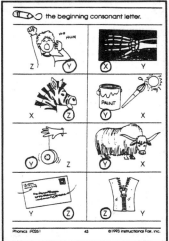

Ending Sounds

Let's try something different. Can you tell the ending sound?

Cup has the ending sound of p. ___ the pictures with the same ending sound.

cup

___ the ending sound of g or m for each picture. ___ the pictures.

rug gum pig

egg dog flag

ham log arm

Ending and Beginning T

Does it end or begin with t?

___ a t on the left if the picture has the beginning sound of t. ___ a t on the right if the picture has the ending sound of t.

(carrot, tulip, goat, pie, tent pictures)

Ending Sounds N, S, L, R

Put on your listening ears. Listen to the ending sound of n or s.

___ the consonant letters. ___ lines from each picture to its ending sound.

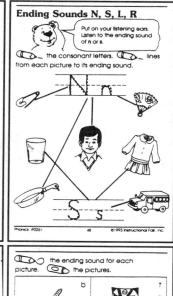

___ the consonant letters. ___ lines from each picture to its ending sound.

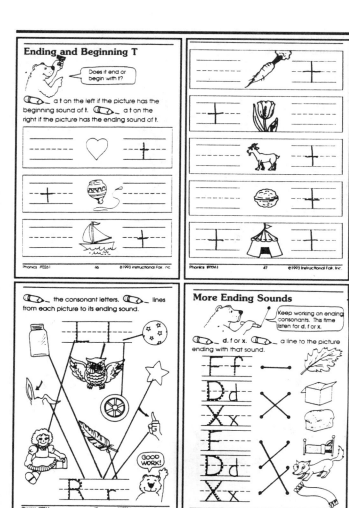

GOOD WORK!

More Ending Sounds

Keep working on ending consonants. This time listen for d, f or x.

___ d, f or x. ___ a line to the picture ending with that sound.

F f
D d
X x
F f
D d
X x

___ the ending sound for each picture. ___ the pictures.

Beginning and Ending Sounds

Say the name of each picture. Fill in the missing letter with the beginning or ending sound.

desk   leaf
fox   corn
mitten pig

---

b ee   sun
hand   ring
queen   goat

___ a picture. ___ the letters it begins and ends with.

Review Beginning and Ending Sounds

Say the name of each picture. ___ the beginning sound with red. ___ the ending sound with blue.

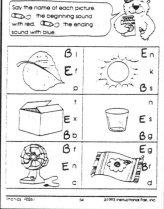

B f / E t / g   E p / B j

B b / m / E d   B f / x / E k

g / B f / E n   B v / E n

B p / E g / w   B h / E t / n

Review Beginning and Ending Sounds

the beginning and ending letter of each word.

log   van

web   yard

boot   leg

hat   bug

fox   pig

can   bib

Review Beginning and Ending Sounds

Say the name of the picture. Listen to the beginning and ending sounds. the word.

pig   pin   fat   fan

bag   bat   bell   beg

hot   hop   bus   bug

pan   pal   ham   hat

cat   cab   ran   rat

cup   cub   sub   sun

pin   pit   rug   run

Word Recognition

Try reading these words. Change the beginning sounds.

Say the name of the picture. Listen to the beginning and ending sounds. a line from the word to the correct picture.

pill

bill

hill

sill

Look at the picture. names of things in the picture listed below. the picture.

king   ring   wing

bing   sing   ding

Initial Blends BR and CR

Can you put these two consonants together to make different words?

Say brick. the br consonant blend.

br   br

br   br

the pictures that begin with the sound like

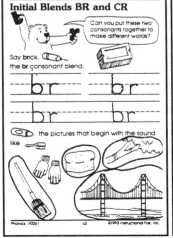

Say crayon. the cr consonant blend.

cr   cr

cr   cr

the pictures that begin with the sound like

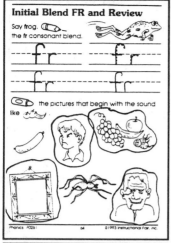

Initial Blend FR and Review

Say frog.
the fr consonant blend.

fr   fr

fr   fr

the pictures that begin with the sound like

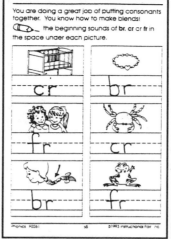

You are doing a great job of putting consonants together. You know how to make blends!

the beginning sounds of **br**, **cr** or **fr** in the space under each picture.

cr   br

fr   cr

br   fr

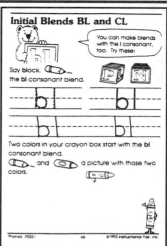

Initial Blends BL and CL

You can make blends with the **l** consonant, too. Try these!

Say block.
the bl consonant blend.

bl   bl

bl   bl

Two colors in your crayon box start with the **bl** consonant blend.

_____ and _____ a picture with those two colors.

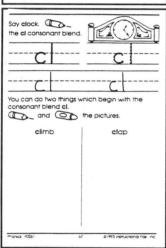

Say clock.
the cl consonant blend.

cl   cl

cl   cl

You can do two things which begin with the consonant blend **cl**.

_____ and _____ the pictures.

climb   clap

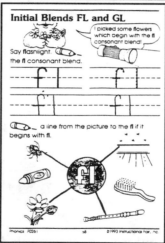

Initial Blends FL and GL

Say flashlight.
the fl consonant blend.

I picked some flowers which begin with the **fl** consonant blend!

fl   fl

fl   fl

_____ a line from the picture to the **fl** if it begins with **fl**.

Say glasses.
the gl consonant blend.

gl   gl

gl   gl

_____ the children whose names begin with the **gl** blend.

Glenn   Gloria

Frank   Gladys

Glenda   Brett

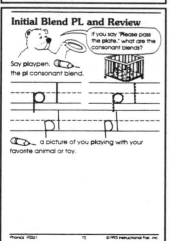

Initial Blend PL and Review

If you say "Please pass the plate," what are the consonant blends?

Say playpen.
the pl consonant blend.

pl   pl

pl   pl

_____ a picture of you **playing** with your favorite animal or toy.

_____ the **pl**, **gl**, **fl**, **cl** or **bl** consonant blend of each picture. _____ the pictures.

clown   flag

block   glove

plane   clip

Review Initial Blends

_____ the pictures that go with each consonant blend.

gr   cr

cl

pl

br   fl

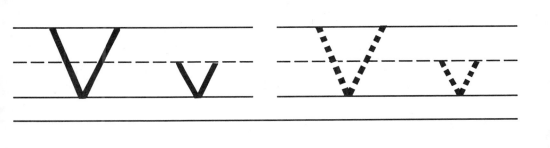

 the pictures that begin with the sound like .

Sound W and Review

I'm looking through a **wide window!**

W w   W w

the pictures that begin with the sound like .

each large and small consonant letter.
a line to the picture that begins with
that sound.

Sounds X and Y

Let's see. The only word I can think of that begins with **x** is **x**-ray.

X x   X x

When you go to the dentist, you get an

-ray

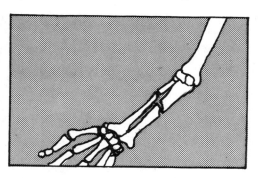

If you break your arm, the doctor takes an

-ray

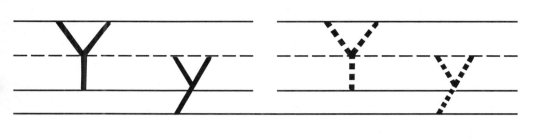

 the pictures that begin with the sound
like .

Sound Z and Review

Z is the last letter in the alphabet! Let's celebrate by going to the **z**oo!

the pictures that begin with the sound like .

the beginning consonant letter.

Z   Y

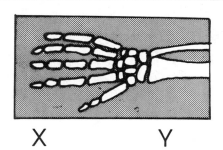

X   Y

X   Z

Y   X

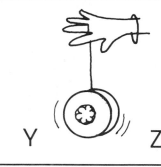

Y   Z

Y   X

Y   Z

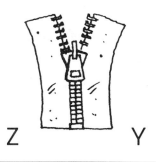

Z   Y

Ending Sounds

Let's try something different. Can you tell the **ending** sound?

Cup has the ending sound of **p**. the pictures with the same ending sound.

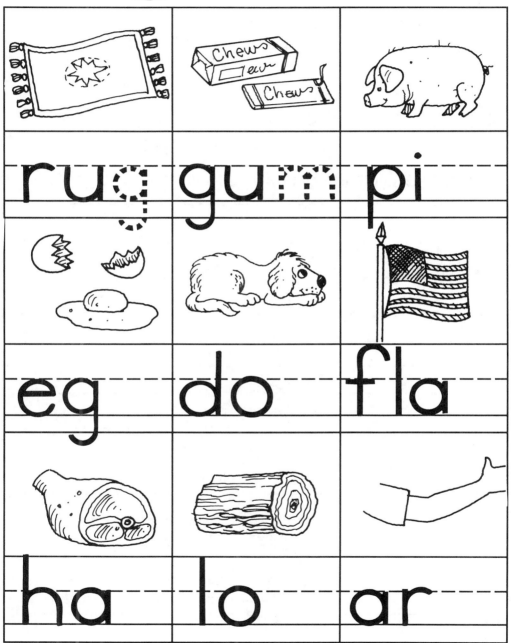

_ the ending sound of **g** or **m** for each picture. the pictures.

rug   gum   pi

eg   do   fla

ha   lo   ar

Ending and Beginning T

Does it end or begin with t?

_ a t on the left if the picture has the beginning sound of t. _ a t on the right if the picture has the ending sound of t.

Ending Sounds N, S, L, R

Put on your listening ears. Listen to the ending sound of **n** or **s**.

_____ the consonant letters. _____ lines from each picture to its ending sound.

___ the consonant letters. ___ lines from each picture to its ending sound.

More Ending Sounds

Keep working on ending consonants. This time listen for **d**, **f** or **x**.

_ **d**, **f** or **x**. _ a line to the picture ending with that sound.

the ending sound for each
picture. the pictures.

	b l (k)		t k b
	k t b		d k b
	b r k		k b x
	k b m		n b k

Beginning and Ending Sounds

Say the name of each picture. Fill in the missing letter with the beginning or ending sound.

desk

fo

mitte

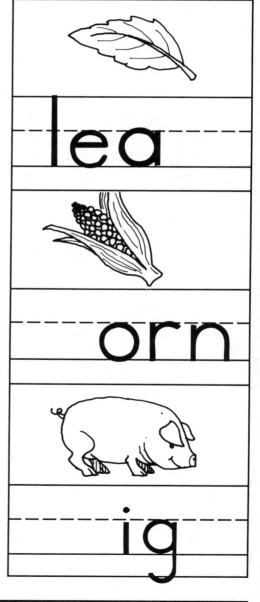

lea

orn

ig

Review Beginning and Ending Sounds

Say the name of each picture. ✏️⟲ the beginning sound with red. ✏️⟲ the ending sound with blue.

l			n
f			k
p			s
t			n
x			s
b			g
f			g
n			r
c			d

	f **t** g		h p **j**
	b m d		**f** x k
	g **f** n		d **v** n
	p g w		**h** t n

Review Beginning and Ending Sounds

✏️ __ the beginning and ending letter of each word.

o c

a

e

ar

o o

e

a

u

o

i

a

i

Review Beginning and Ending Sounds

Say the name of the picture.
Listen to the beginning and
ending sounds.  the word.

(pig) pin	fat fan
bag bat	bell beg
hot hop	bus bug

pan pal	ham hat
cat cab	ran rat
cup cub	sub sun
pin pit	rug run

Word Recognition

Try reading these words. Change the beginning sounds.

Say the name of the picture. Listen to the beginning and ending sounds.  a line from the word to the correct picture.

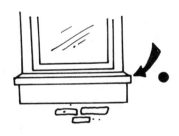 •

• pill

 •

• bill

•

• hill

 •

• sill

Look at the picture. ✎⟳ names of things
in the picture listed below. ⬭ the picture.

| king | ring | wing |
| bing | sing | ding |

Initial Blends BR and CR

Can you put these two consonants together to make different words?

Say **br**ick.
the **br** consonant blend.

br   br

the pictures that begin with the sound
like

Say **cr**ayon.  _____ the **cr** consonant blend.

cr _____ cr

_____ the pictures that begin with the sound like 👑 .

Initial Blend FR and Review

Say **frog**.
the **fr** consonant blend.

f r   f r

the pictures that begin with the sound
like .

You are doing a great job of putting consonants together. You know how to make blends!

 the beginning sounds of **br**, **cr** or **fr** in the space under each picture.

_ _ _ c r _ _ _

_ _ _ _ _ _ _

_ _ _ _ _ _ _

_ _ _ _ _ _ _

_ _ _ _ _ _ _

_ _ _ _ _ _ _

Initial Blends BL and CL

You can make blends with the **l** consonant, too. Try these!

Say **bl**ock.  the **bl** consonant blend.

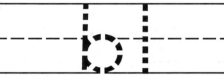

Two colors in your crayon box start with the **bl** consonant blend.

 and a picture with those two colors.

66 ©1993 Instructional Fair, Inc.

Say **cl**ock.  _
the **cl** consonant blend.

c|

You can do two things which begin with the
consonant blend **cl**.

___ and ___ the pictures.

climb   **cl**ap

Initial Blends FL and GL

Say **fl**ashlight. ✏ _
the **fl** consonant blend.

I picked some **flowers**
which begin with the **fl**
consonant blend!

f l

f l

✏ _ a line from the picture to the **fl** if it
begins with **fl**.

Say **gl**asses.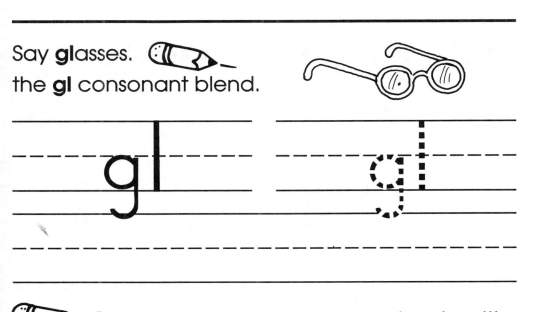
the **gl** consonant blend.

g l

g

 the children whose names begin with
the **gl** blend.

Glenn

Gloria

Frank

Gladys

Glenda

Brett

Initial Blend PL and Review

If you say "**Pl**ease pass the **pl**ate," what are the consonant blends?

Say **pl**aypen. the **pl** consonant blend.

_____ a picture of you **pl**aying with your favorite animal or toy.

_____ the **pl**, **gl**, **fl**, **cl** or **bl** consonant blend of each picture. _____ the pictures.

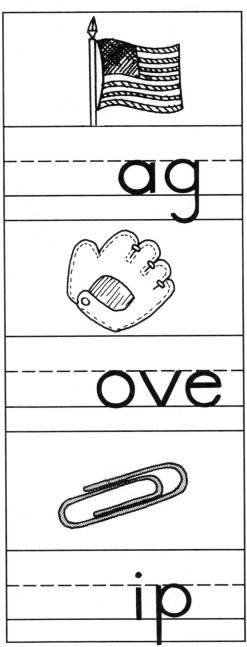

c own

ag

ock

ove

ane

ip

Review Initial Blends

the pictures that go with each consonant blend.

gl	cr
fr	cl
bl	pl
br	fl

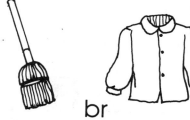

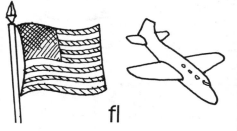